So You're A Good Cook, Now What?

How To Write, Self Publish, Market, and Earn A Lifetime Income From, Your Own Cookbook. For FREE!

Shawn Christopher

[Shawn Hoover]   2

Dedication

This book is dedicated to the love of my life, Shawn Davis Mooney.

Without him, none of this would have been possible.

Forward

I've always been considered a good cook. For as long as I can remember, even back into my childhood. I guess that's my Mom's doing. She was an awesome cook and spent the time to teach an interested young boy how to cook everything from scratch, mostly with home grown and home canned ingredients. Oh the memories.

This book however isn't about my cooking skills. This book is about how, with no money, no job (at the time), and no formal writing skills, I was able to write, self publish, market, and earn a monthly income off of my original recipes.

It was a learning experience for sure. I had the idea to write a cookbook a little over 10 years before actually writing one. I kept hitting the same old obstacles that I'm sure many of you reading this have hit. Like finding a niche that's not so saturated with cookbooks on the subject that they are all selling two for a dollar on the cart outside the front door of the local book store. Like getting a publisher to even glance your way since nobody knows who you are yet.

I Googled "How-To" books on writing, cookbooks, publishing, etc., I contacted publishers, I followed many different and sometimes conflicting advice from everybody on the internet that claimed to be a successful author. I spent years running in circles with brief periods of "giving up". I couldn't figure out how to make money from my cooking and everybody wanted to sell me something that promised to make me an author.

It was when I watched a most inspiring movie, "Julie & Julia" that it clicked. It was like a light bulb went off inside of me. I immediately began Googling how to write a blog. Where to start? What platform to use? What specific to write about? Honestly, there were so many questions I felt overwhelmed by the whole idea of it all and a couple of different times I put it on the back burner and went about my daily life.

You know something is important to you when you can't stop thinking about it. When it constantly keeps filtering into your thoughts and soon this whisper in the back of your mind becomes a shout and... well... back to researching and writing. As you probably have guessed, since you're reading this, I did finally write and publish my cookbook, and then another, and now I intend to teach you how to do the same, not for free, but with the tiny investment of $5 or less you can learn to do everything I did for free to go from an unknown home cook to a globally recognized author of cookbooks that continue to sell.

This book will lay out for you step-by-step how I went from a nobody that cooks for my family to a published author of two cookbooks with international sales earning a monthly income. I started with just an idea, some recipes, and no money and went on to retire at 42 to live off of the income from the royalties. Retirement is boring and I've recently opened a small business to occupy my time but that's another story.

I hope you enjoy this book and become a successful cookbook author from reading it. This book contains everything that I wish someone would have shared with me when I first started contemplating the idea of writing my own cookbook.

From the telling of my story, it is my hope that you can use the information to do exactly what I did and I hope you become even more successful than me as a cookbook author.

Contents

Chapter 1: The Concept: What's Your Specialty?

Chapter 2: The Blog: Choosing Your Platform.

Chapter 3: Social Media: Building an Audience.

**Chapter 4: Immediate and Secondary Income: Ads and
Affiliate Programs**

Chapter 5: Self Publishing: Digital and Print

Chapter 1

The Concept: What's Your Specialty?

What's your specialty? It's great to find a cookbook niche that you are not only very knowledgeable about but excel in. It's a good idea to research your specialty on the web to see how saturated the market is. Don't be daunted though by an over saturated market if you think that you have a fresh voice and a fresh concept or a unique take on a certain type of food. Lord knows that I jumped into an over saturated market. My cookbook specialty is gluten-free baking and even in this over saturated market I found my voice and carved out my niche. It's a big world but you can make room for yourself and get your voice heard. If I was able to do it, you can too. Just follow my advice.

So, What's your specialty? Gluten-Free, Allergen Friendly? Comfort Food? Fusion? Something more specific? Something less specific?

There are a lot of questions you should ask yourself before you get started to find your specific niche. What makes you buy the cookbooks you buy? Would your cookbook appeal to you in the store? Is this the kind of book you could see in a bookstore?

Look at the newest cooking trends. Is there something trending that you are good at? What's the next big trend? Could it be your specialty?

The best way for me to teach you how to do it is to tell you exactly how I did it. I originally thought of writing a Vegan cookbook, but after spending 3 years as a Vegan it just never manifested so I went on with my life and put the "cookbook author" idea on the shelf for another day.

My husband was diagnosed with Celiac disease and the following few months of freaking out about what he could eat without getting sick combined with being grossed out by the texture and taste of gluten-free commercially available foods in the store.

I had that "Aha" moment you always hear about. That moment of clarity. An epiphany, if you will. "I can cook, surely I can make a better gluten-free version of _____. " (fill in the blank).

This realization was inspiring. I went out and bought every different gluten-free flour I could find to begin my kitchen experiments. I was prepared for long grueling work, but as it turned out, I nailed most recipes first try. I chalk that up to my cooking training from my mom combined with a rather copious amount of online research and reading on the subject.

What now? How do I keep track of my progress and my recipes? How do I organize? How do I get feedback and or build a customer base to insure sales?

The answer to these questions and many more came with a coincidental and very inspiring night of Netflix. Snuggled on the couch, we watched "Julie & Julia".

I highly recommend it.

While this movie is a true story, it's not about a cookbook author writing a cookbook, but rather it's about a blogger named Julie who reaches out to the world through a blog she writes about her adventures cooking her way through a Julia Child's cookbook.

The movie turned on a light inside of me and I began researching that night how to write and turn a profit from a cooking blog. I was still thinking I needed to raise enough money to self publish my cookbook and was not yet aware of how to do it for free. We're still at the beginning of this journey.

I discovered I had an innate, oh let's use "knack" for lack of a better word, for creating awesome gluten-free baked goods with the texture and taste of their gluten-full counterparts. I discovered this only when forced to by circumstances (my husband having celiac disease).

When you've found your niche, discovered your cooking specialty, have a solid concept, and are ready to move forward on the path to becoming a cookbook author it's time to research, and create a blog. I cover this thoroughly in the next chapter.

Chapter 2

The Blog: Choosing Your Platform

So by this point in the process you've chosen your specialty in cooking, have a solid concept of the book you want to write and are wondering "Where is a good place to start?". If you have the money you can write your book now and pay to have it self published through several different companies. I had a friend do this and it cost him out of pocket $7,000 when all was said and done. It's now 8 years later and he has yet to recoup that money.

In contrast, I spent nothing and my first months royalty check was for more money than my friend made in his first year with his book through a publishing company. The difference was in our royalty percentage per copy sold. He got something like .07% of the sale of each book, I get usually 70% on digital sales and roughly 10-20% of print sales.

You can even shop around to a few publishers with your idea at this point, but when no one's ever heard of you it's hard to get a publisher to take notice. This book is about how to do it for FREE and make money not spend it, so let's focus on that.

The next FREE step to get you started in the process is selecting a blogging platform. That's just a fancy way of saying "Which company will you be using to write and publish your blog on the internet?" The two major ones are Blogger and WordPress. I've had people sing the praises of both as well as point out the flaws in both. After much debate, I chose Blogger so this is the one I'll talk about in this book. It's simpler to get started and the templates are FREE.

I chose Blogger for the following reasons:

1. It's Free.
2. I already use Google Chrome, Google Picasa, Google Doc's, Google AdWords, etc. and it integrates with all of these seamlesly.
3. It's super easy to set up and get started.
4. Google Adwords (more about this in chapter 4)
5. It was created and is owned by the largest search engine company out there and has excellent Search Engine Optimization.

It's a good idea to buy a Domain name for your blog {www.yourname.com} but that can cost you somewhere between $5-$20 and this is a tutorial for doing this for FREE.

Blogger will let you publish under a dot.blogspot name {www.yourname.blogspot.com} This makes the process completely FREE and is how I originally started out. Later I bought a domain name (a .com) with some of the generated income and added it to my blog.

Google's Blogger is a super easy (and FREE) blogging platform. Just answer a few questions to get started and start posting. Pictures can be uploaded easily and are kept in a Picasa account (Google's online photo storage) for you to use later if needed. They've recently changed the name from "Picasa" to "Google+ Photos" but it hasn't really caught on yet.

Log into Blogger and create an account. Follow all the prompts and fill in the blanks. (name of blog, subtitle, description, etc.)

I started mine with a recipe, some pictures, a step by step photo essay of how to prepare and cook the recipe. I think I did 3 or 4 blog recipe's that first day on blogger. It was easy once I settled into my groove and figured out how to do it.

I decided to post at least one recipe or product review per week although in reality I posted much more than that. The blog became a way to categorize and organize my recipes while engaging readers and building a fan base and at the same time honing my writing skills. I turned my kitchen into a photo shoot each and every night when cooking dinner or trying new recipes out on my family. I made sure to photograph each step in the process so that if the recipe was a success, it could easily be turned into a blog post later that evening.

I didn't work at the time so I offset the price of ingredients by setting up at a local farmer's market and selling my gluten-free baked goods once a week. (I strongly recommend this if your specialty involves baked goods of any type to help test and perfect recipes as well as build a local following). This not only gave me opportunity to make some extra money, it helped get my name out there (I packaged the goods with the blog name), it also gave me the opportunity to perfect some cookie and bread recipes by baking large quantities of them in bulk and selling them to willing taste testers.   These recipes made their way onto the blog too.

The recipe creation part of my cookbook plan of action was coming together nicely but I needed to build a bigger online following. I did this through social media networking which will be discussed at length in the next chapter.

Chapter 3

Social Media: Building an Audience

How can you grow a fan base fast?

Social media like Facebook, Twitter, and Google+ can rapidly increase the number of people that know who you are. When you get to the step where you publish your book, you want as large of a fan base as you possibly can so you have a lot of sales.

Here's how I did it.

First I created a **Facebook** business page for my blog. I searched on Facebook for pages, groups , and businesses similar to mine and "liked" them as my page. I then created a **Twitter** account for the blog. I then joined **Networked Blogs.** Networked blogs is a very useful tool. You can connect it to your blog, and to your Facebook account, and to your Twitter account. Then every time you post a new blog, Networked Blogs automatically posts it to your Facebook and Twitter for you. This will help you engage more people in less time, remember to use this FREE tool.

Use Facebook to engage people more than just sharing your blog posts. I used mine to post a lot of very well staged and tantalizing pictures of completed recipes, plated desserts, or cookies cooling on a rack that helped to advertise upcoming blog posts and generate buzz. Social media platforms like Facebook work on connections and interactions so each picture I posted I tagged the picture with my page name, then tagged it with the Facebook pages of the companies that produced the ingredients I used in the recipe. This is an important step. This shared the picture with the pages I tagged, which in turn shared it with their Facebook fans too. Some of the fans will "Like" your page, which is the reason for doing this in the first place. Some pages have tens of thousands of fans, some have hundreds of thousands. That's a tremendous amount of potential readers/fans.

After awhile the social media operators for the products you've been tagging in your pictures will start to take notice. I was asked to guest blog for my favorite gluten-free flour company a couple of times, not for pay, and while they did thank me with free products the exposure was the real payment.

Facebook provides an excellent platform for asking and answering questions from fans. I like to engage fans as much as possible.

Search for businesses, groups, and pages similar to your theme or specialty and "Like" them. Once you've liked a substantial number of pages, check your news feed. "Share" posts from pages that have information you think you're readers will like. Comment on posts, (as your business page not your personal Facebook). This gets your blogs name out there in front of more people. Remember it's all about the number of potential book buyers.

It's also a good idea to contact (via Facebook) your favorite companies that make the products you use most often and/or like the best, in a private message on Facebook and pitch a "Give-away" of their products on your blog. They usually are extremely happy to provide you with product prizes to give away to your readers. Generally I get compensated with FREE product for doing this also as a bonus. For example, I contacted a famous Oregon based flour manufacturer and asked if I could hold a Give-Away of a 4 pack of my 4 favorite flours from their company. They provided me with Two 4 pack gift sets for giving away on my blog and an additional 4 pack for my own use. Giveaways really attract fans fast.

To run a Giveaway on your blog it's easy. The simplest way is to create an acount with a company called "Rafflecopter" .   Rafflecopter provides you with a FREE widget that allows people to enter once or multiple entries, your choice. You can set entries based on answering a question or based on a task that must be completed to gain the entry. Examples of tasks are: "Like us on Facebook" or "Follow us on Twitter" or "Leave a comment" these are the most popular ones I use to gain followers from entries.   Rafflecopter comes in a widget that is easily copy and pasted into your next blog post. It tracks all entries and tasks and picks the winner on the specified date (you set the length of the contest and the terms).

I cross post and share the Rafflecopter Giveaway post as often as possible to my social media pages. People love FREE contest giveaways.

At this point you might be thinking this book is supposed to be about self publishing my cookbook, what is all this about blogging and Facebook pages? That's a good point. All of this blogging and social media is essential to building yourself a known persona with which to publish your cookbook under and have a fan base already in place that will immediately begin purchasing your cookbook as soon as you get it published.

What about Twitter? I just don't do much with Twitter myself but it is another essential tool. Networked Blogs (we spoke of them earlier) automatically posts every blog post to Twitter and every Facebook post to Twitter for me so there really isn't a great need for me to go to Twitter and tweet anything else, yet.

Since this chapter is about using social media to get your name out there and build a fan base, here is another idea for you. I also registered my blog with a website named CookEatShare, another great FREE resource, which featured my blog for awhile as well as sent tons of traffic (visitors) to my blog. You might have guessed by the name that it is a recipe sharing website. It turned out to be an invaluable tool for getting my name out there, I highly recommend registering your blog with them. They will give you a small widget of code to copy and paste onto your website that advertises them and you. I got tons of traffic referred to my website from doing this.

Now it's time to make some money.

Chapter 4

Immediate and Secondary Income: Ads and Affiliate Programs

This chapter is dedicated to generating some income with your blog. I'll cover some important steps to make sure your blog starts earning you some income, no matter how small, immediately that you can grow into a sizable monthly deposit into your bank account. The goal is, of course, to self publish your cookbook and earn income from the royalties but while waiting for that point in time you could be generating some additional income. It can and will, in these first few months, earn enough to cover the expense of buying a Domain Name (a dot com).

Ads

Advertisements on your blog can earn you some monthly income. The more visitors you have to your website, the more money you can earn. Ads generally pay on a CPM (cost per thousand page views) For instance if you place an ad on your blog that pays $8.00 CPM and you have 10,000 visitors to your blog that month, they will pay you $80.00 for that month.

One good source for ads is Foodie Blogroll. Google them and sign your blog up. They will provide you with simple copy and paste ads to place on your blogs sidebar or header. (really simple to do with step-by-step instructions provided). They do have placement requirements though, like the sidebar ad needs to be placed "above the fold" . This is an old newspaper term meaning the ad has to be visible on the side of your page or top of your page to anyone that has just logged on.

The viewer should not have to scroll down the page to see the advertisement. This will be explained in depth by Foodie Blogroll when you sign up. I got some handsome payouts from this company during the first year of my blog.

Another great source of advertising income is Google Adwords. Google Adwords is easy to sign up for and can be done right from your Blogger dashboard when setting up your blog. They place ads in your sidebar and at the end of each blog as well as in your RSS feeds if you want. They have no requirements as to placement so they can be, and most often are, placed below the fold. Google Adwords generates and pays you via check or direct deposit only when the total exceeds $100.00. Don't worry, I got paid several times a year, it did not take long to reach the minimum payment threshold.

You can also approach companies directly for advertising on your blog or for blog sponsorship once you've established yourself over a few months.

Choose your favorite products and companies. Make sure you like their products and use them often and make sure it's something you don't mind putting your name and reputation behind.

Affiliates

Signing up to be an affiliate for a company is a great idea to generate more monthly income without any extra work. There seems to be no end to companies that offer affiliate programs out there but I'm only going to discuss two of them. The ones that generated the quickest and most income.

Amazon.com Affiliate Program is essential, especially if you are planning to self publish your own book. Here's how the Amazon Affiliate Program works for me. With every blog post I take a lot of pictures of the preparation at different steps in the process of completing the recipe. People like to see visuals of the food being prepared and it helps them compare their personal results with yours at every step. The pictures often show my stand mixer, or my mixing bowl set, or a designer whisk, or my baking pans, mixing bowls, etc. etc.

I then go to Amazon Associate Central and use the tools there to browse for the products I use in my kitchen that got featured in the picture I took for my blog. Amazon lets me create a link to that product on their website and place that link in the body of my blog post (or wherever I like it to be).

When a reader clicks on the link it takes them to Amazon.com to buy the item. If they buy it, you get a percentage of the sale. Even better, they don't even have to buy what you just linked to. They could buy something else entirely once they get to Amazon's website, you still get the percentage of anything they buy because you sent them to Amazon from your blog site. Even better still, clicking on the Affiliate product link from your blog puts a "cookie" in their internet browser that lasts for 60 days. If at any time over the next 60 days they return to Amazon.com and buy anything, you get a percentage of the sale. It adds up fast as you can well imagine.

Once you self publish your book, you can use Amazon Affiliate links to advertise your book to the public on all of your social media and on your blog, then you not only get your usual royalty for the sale of your book, you also get an additional percentage from the affiliate link. Bonus!

Google Affiliate Links are something you can access directly from your blog dashboard and you can add links directly to your post from blogger. It's very easy to set up and builds income fast. Select "monetize" on your blogger dashboard to get started and follow the prompts. I often sell things through Google Affiliate Links and income earned from these links combine with your Google Adwords totals, which make that amount grow faster and make it's way into your bank account faster.

I should mention that mixed in with all my recipes on the blog I did product reviews (of products I used anyways). A few of these reviews garnered the attention of corporate reps and that had an unexpected result. I started receiving requests to do "compensated" product reviews. Most would simply send me product or coupons for FREE products and ask me to review them honestly. A few offered me money to "guest blog" on their website blog, this usually paid around $200-$250 for a blog post. I'm sure if you mix in a few posts that are product reviews, you too will get free food, coupons, and cash offers.

Chapter 5

Self Publishing: Digital and Print

The entire process leading up to this point took me 1 year. I think it should take you at least that amount of time too, to insure it works as good for you as it has for me. My blog had made it up to 40,000 visitors per month from all over the world. More than one reader had suggested I write a cookbook. I had thousands of followers on Facebook and Twitter and it was time.

There are companies out there that will, without any effort on your part, turn your blog into a book. This is expensive and not really practical as a self publishing option.

I began by researching FREE Templates for cookbook writing online and hit a few dead ends.

The best I found and the one I used, as well as the one I am using right now, was a FREE template for "Kindle Books" from Apache Open Office. I immediately downloaded Apache Open Office and the template and set out to write my first cookbook. The great part was that I already had a years worth of recipes organized and categorized on my blog. A cookbook you write doesn't necessarily have to be 100% NEW content as long as it is YOUR content, it can be a percentage of new recipes sprinkled in with some of your old favorite blog recipes revamped.

There are still a lot of people that aren't computer savvy and prefer books over a computer screen. I sell quite a few books to people that are buying it for someone as a gift too, so including some of your best recipes from your blog is a good idea. I would suggest making the recipe and shooting some new pictures of the finished product to freshen it up a bit for print.

OK, Now I think I've made it easier for you to organize and write your cookbook. Have fun with it, be precise, have someone proof read it for you and encourage them to give you honest feedback.

Now we'll skip ahead in this to when the book is written, and you're happy with it.

How do you publish it? Well first off go to Kindle Direct Publishing (www.kdp.com) and create an account. Once you've created your account it's as simple as following the onscreen prompts and guidelines, selecting your price structure, (I suggest sticking within the 70% payout structure, again this is what I did.) and publishing it.

While you are waiting for the website to proofread and approve your book for publishing, which may take a few days, you can begin the process of publishing the print version, also for FREE.

Make a FREE account with Create Space (www.createspace.com).   Follow the onscreen prompts and upload your book to be published. This is an awesome "print on demand" publisher. This is also the website I got a link to a FREE book cover designer. You can always just Google "Free Book Cover Designer" and choose one from the plentiful list. You'll need a book cover picture to upload in the publishing process.

Both Create Space and Kindle Direct Publishing will require the cover picture uploaded. Both will also ask for your bank account information and by all means give it to them, it is completely safe and that's the best way for them to pay you. If this step really bothers you, you can opt for payment via check, then they only need your address. You will, however, have to give them your Social Security Number because the income you earn is taxable and you will receive 1099's at the end of the each year.

Now you are published. The rest is all marketing.

Let's recap:

1. Choose your niche, your specialty, your idea.

Decide on your specialty. What is your cookbook going to be about? Do the research and put in the time to make sure there is an audience for your book.

2. Start your blog.

Blogger by Google is what I know best and what I selected, but do some research on your own and see which one works best for you. Title the blog with your online persona/cookbook title. Post often (a minimum of once per week).

3. Social Media.

Create Facebook and Twitter accounts and then connect them to each other and to your blog with Networked Blogs. Use these social media accounts to engage readers and acquire new readers by reaching out to companies and products. Host giveaways and even start doing product review posts.

4. Income.

Let companies put Ads on your blog. I suggest Foodie Blogroll, but there are others out there. Do a little research to see which one best fits you. Set up affiliate accounts. I originally started with many, but narrowed it down to Amazon.com and Google Affiliates.

Well, that's it. Short but sweet. The information contained here is exactly how I did it. I started out as nobody and am now recognized internationally as a gluten-free cookbook author with sales in every market Amazon.com serves.

I am 100% positive that with this information and my story that you too can earn a monthly income from your recipes. I did.

Write more than one. Each year write another. My first was a tutorial on gluten-free bread making, now that's specific! My second was a guide to throwing a "celiac-safe" holiday party. You could write and publish one cookbook a year for 5 years and have more than enough residual income to semi-retire and spend your days creating more recipes for more books, or simply marketing the ones you already wrote.

I wrote my two cookbooks in one year and that might have been rushing things a bit. Take your time and enjoy the process.

About The Author

Shawn Christopher started life out after college as an artist and a choreographer. Through some unexpected life events he turned his lifelong passion for cooking and baking into a full time career. With a specialty cooking blog and two cookbooks published he decided to teach others to do what he has done, which is make a living from royalties off the sales of the cookbook and the advertisements on the blog. Shawn currently is semi-retired at the ripe old age of 44 in a sunny coastal town in southwest Florida and enjoys writing and cooking.